FOR THE LOVE OF
St. Pete

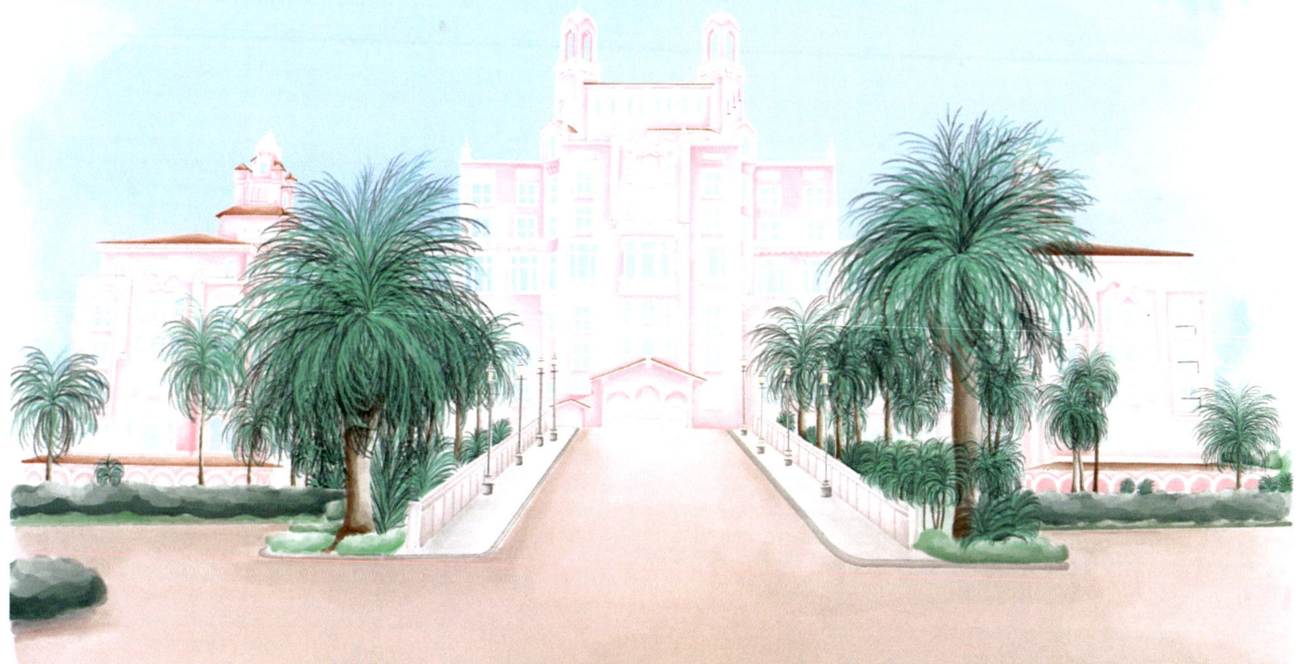

Written by Seth Sjostrom
Artwork by Michele Sjostrom

FOR THE LOVE OF St. Pete

Written by Seth Sjostrom
Artwork by Michele Sjostrom

wolfprintMedia, LLC
Hernando Beach, FL 34607

Hardcover
ISBN-13: 978-1-960501-33-2

1. Fiction. 2. Title - For the Love of St. Pete 3. Series -
For the Love of

First edition 2025.
wolfprintMedia is a trademark of wolfprintMedia, LLC. Postcard Press is an imprint of wolfprintMedia.

For information regarding bulk purchases, please contact wolfprintMedia, LLC, at
wolfprint@hotmail.com.

United States of America

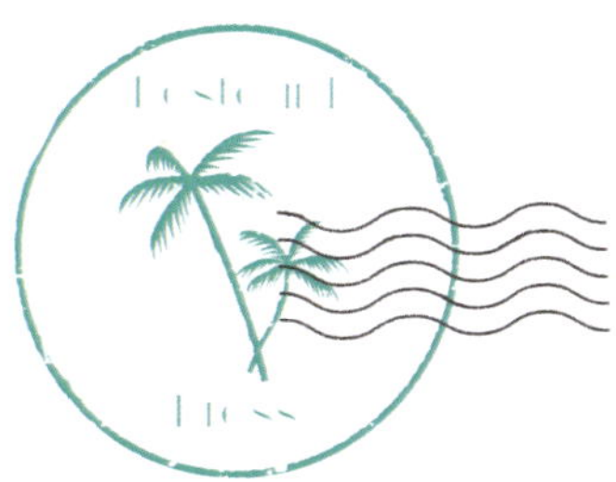

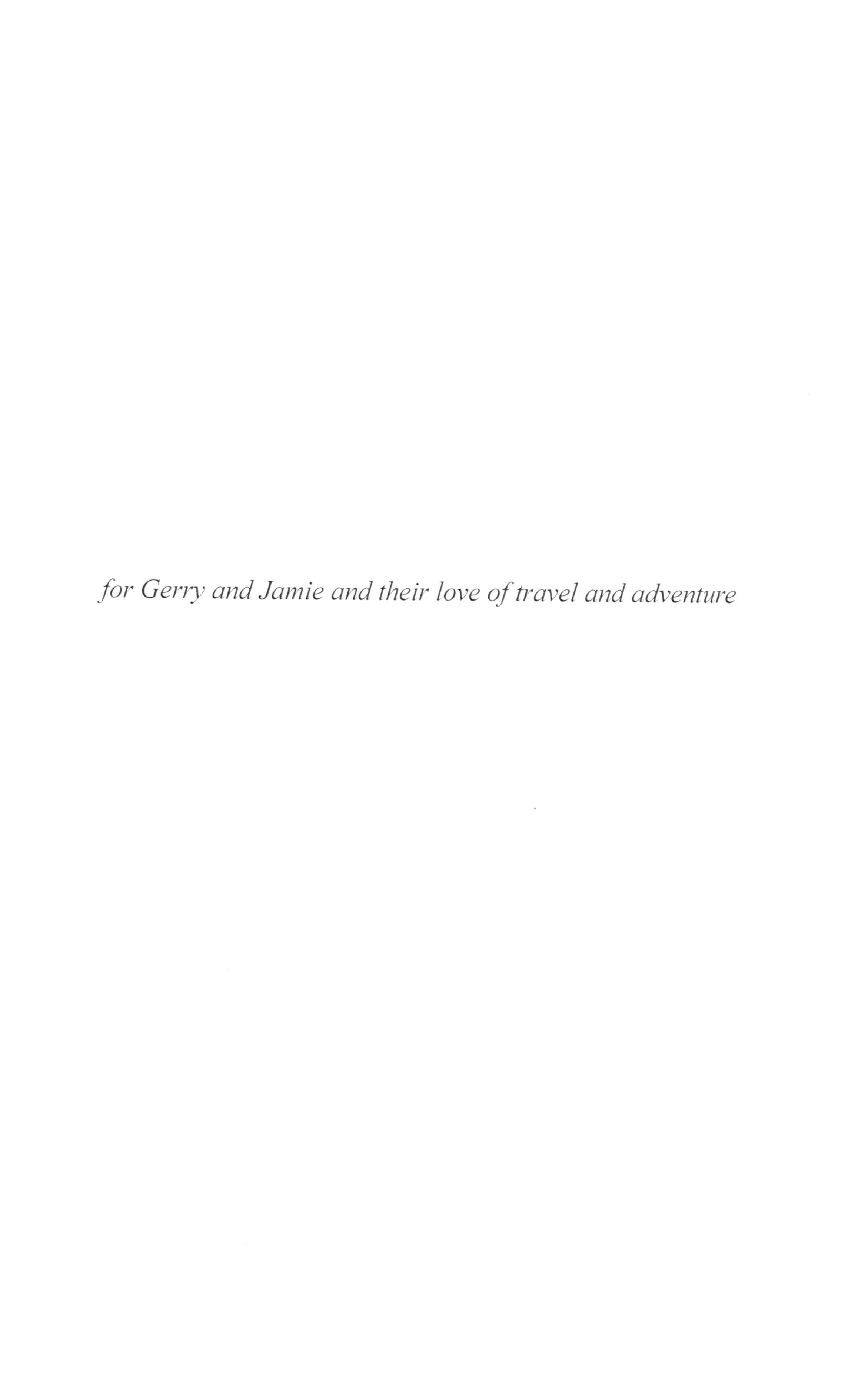

for Gerry and Jamie and their love of travel and adventure

For the L♥ve of
St. Pete

Whether you live here or just come to visit, there is a lot to love about St. Petersburg.

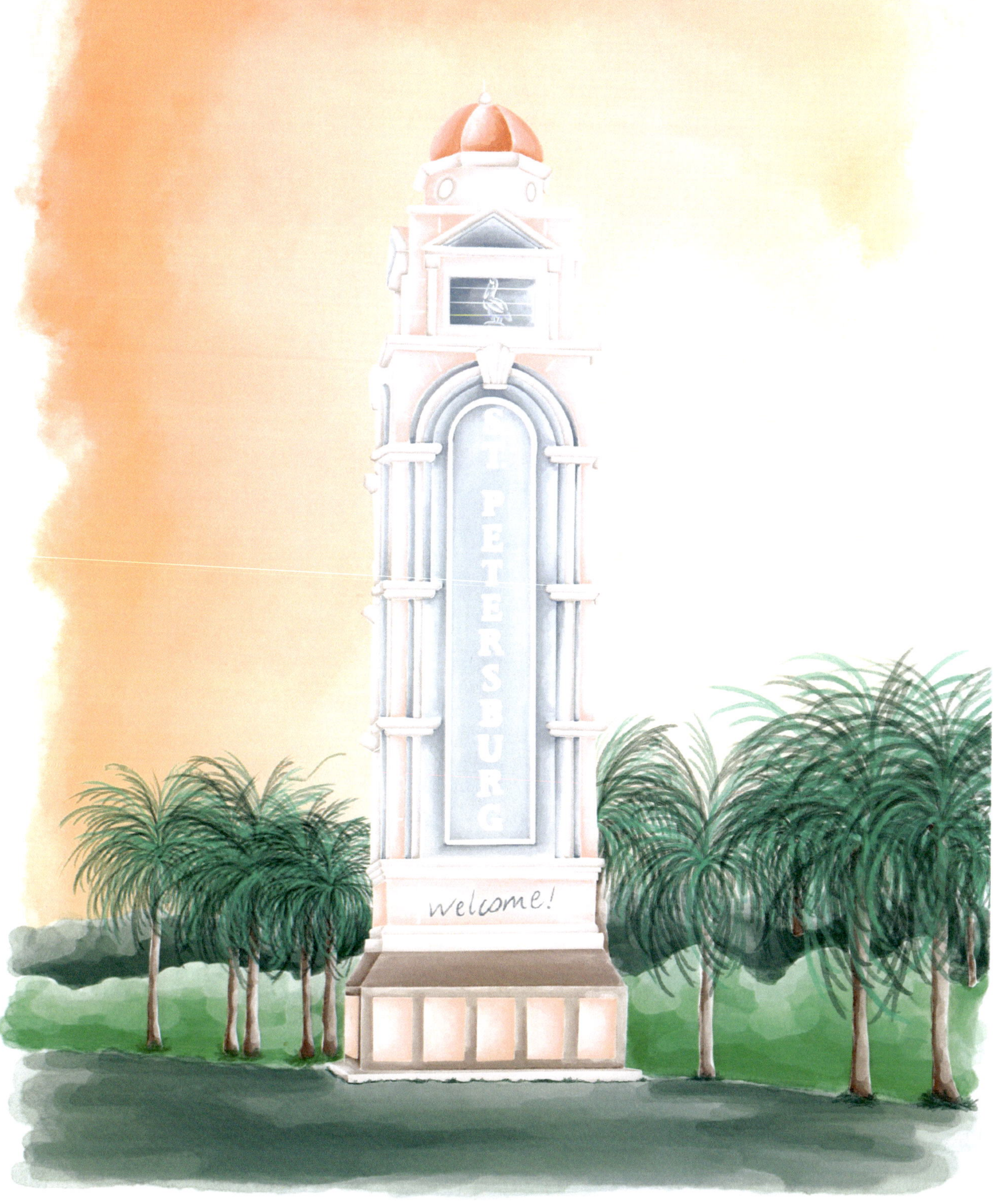

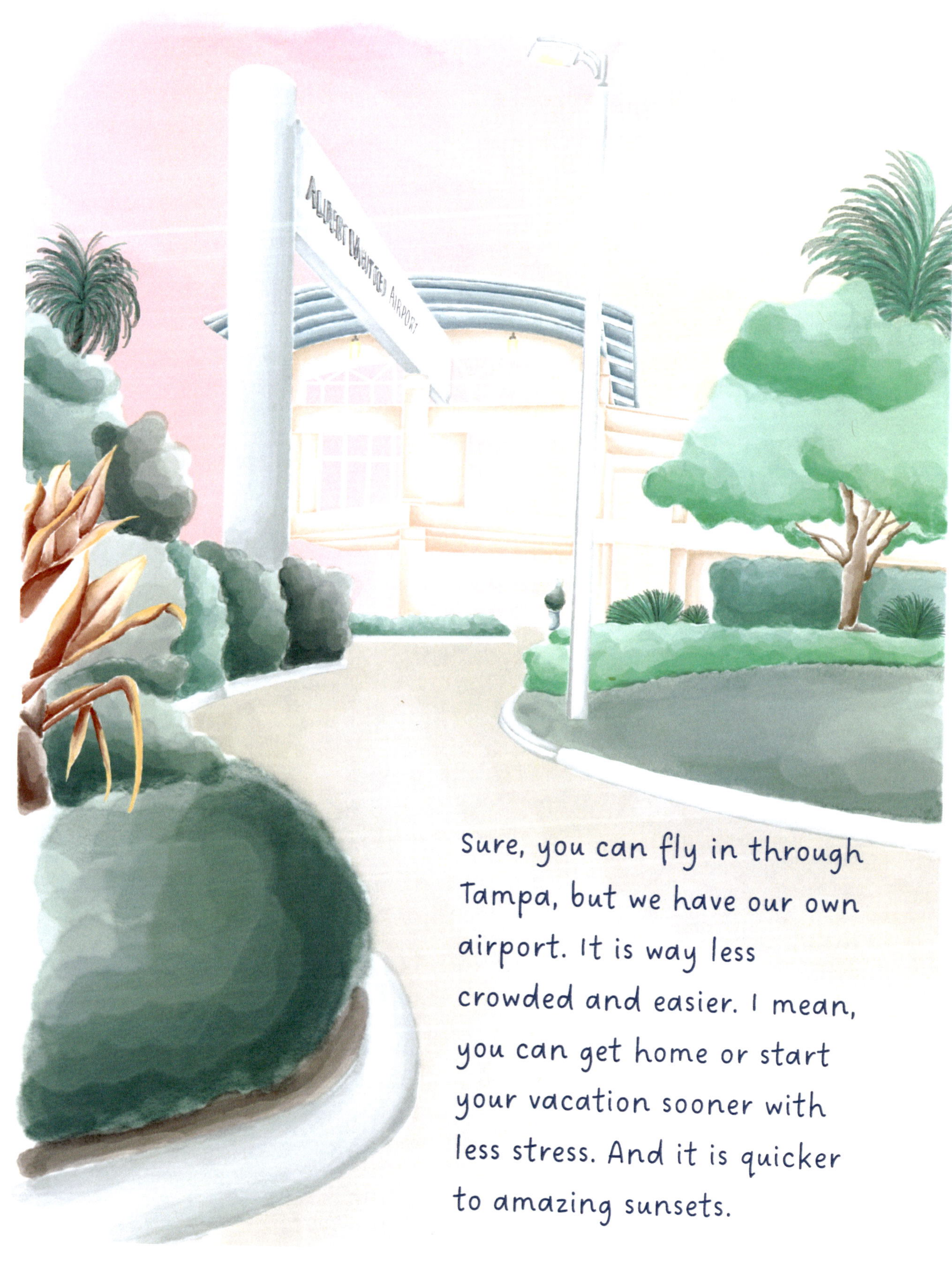

Sure, you can fly in through Tampa, but we have our own airport. It is way less crowded and easier. I mean, you can get home or start your vacation sooner with less stress. And it is quicker to amazing sunsets.

Time and nature molds everything on earth, including the skyline. Tropicana Field and its big dome has been a feature of St. Pete for a long time. Unfortunately, it met with one hurricane too many.

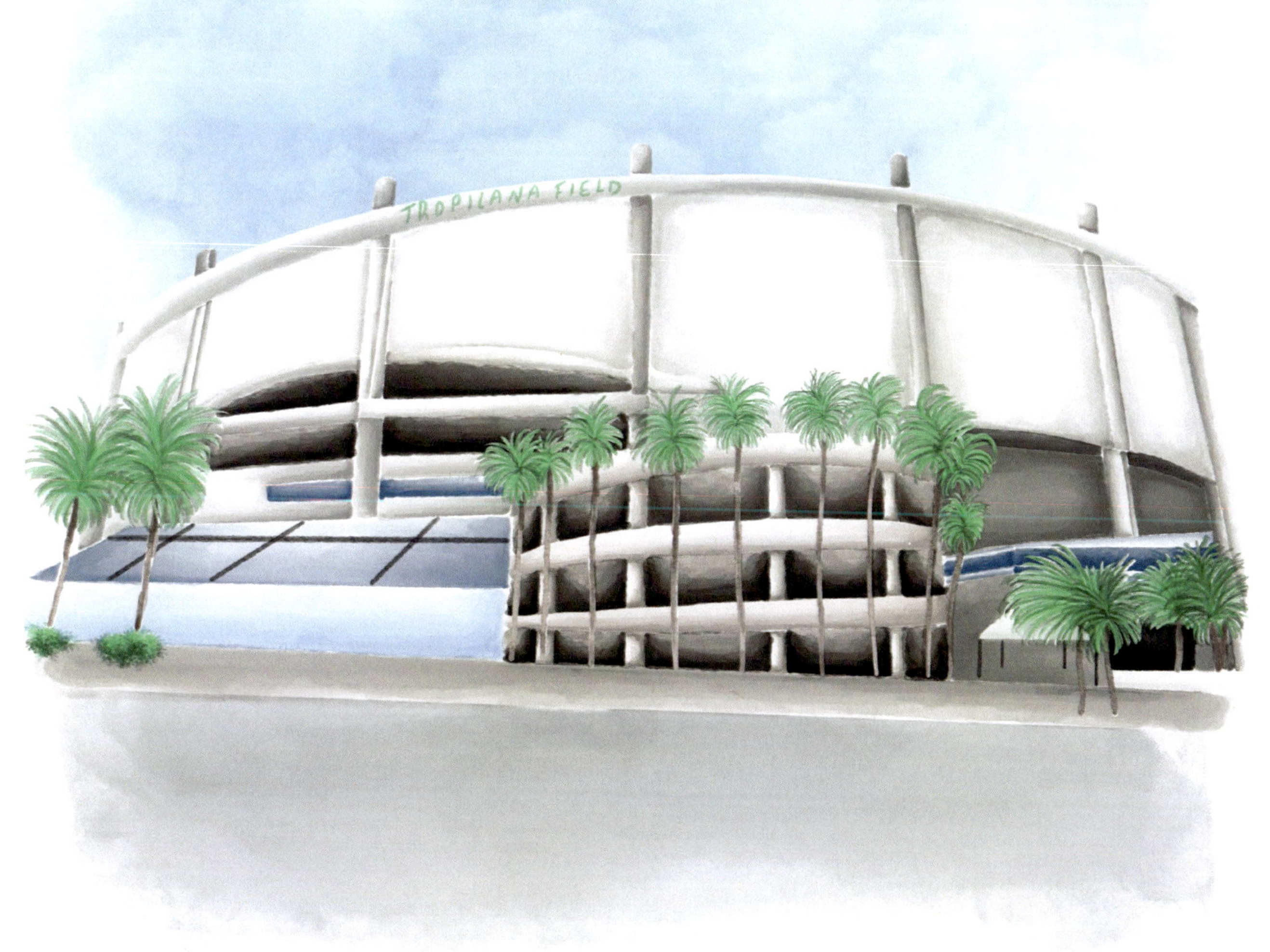

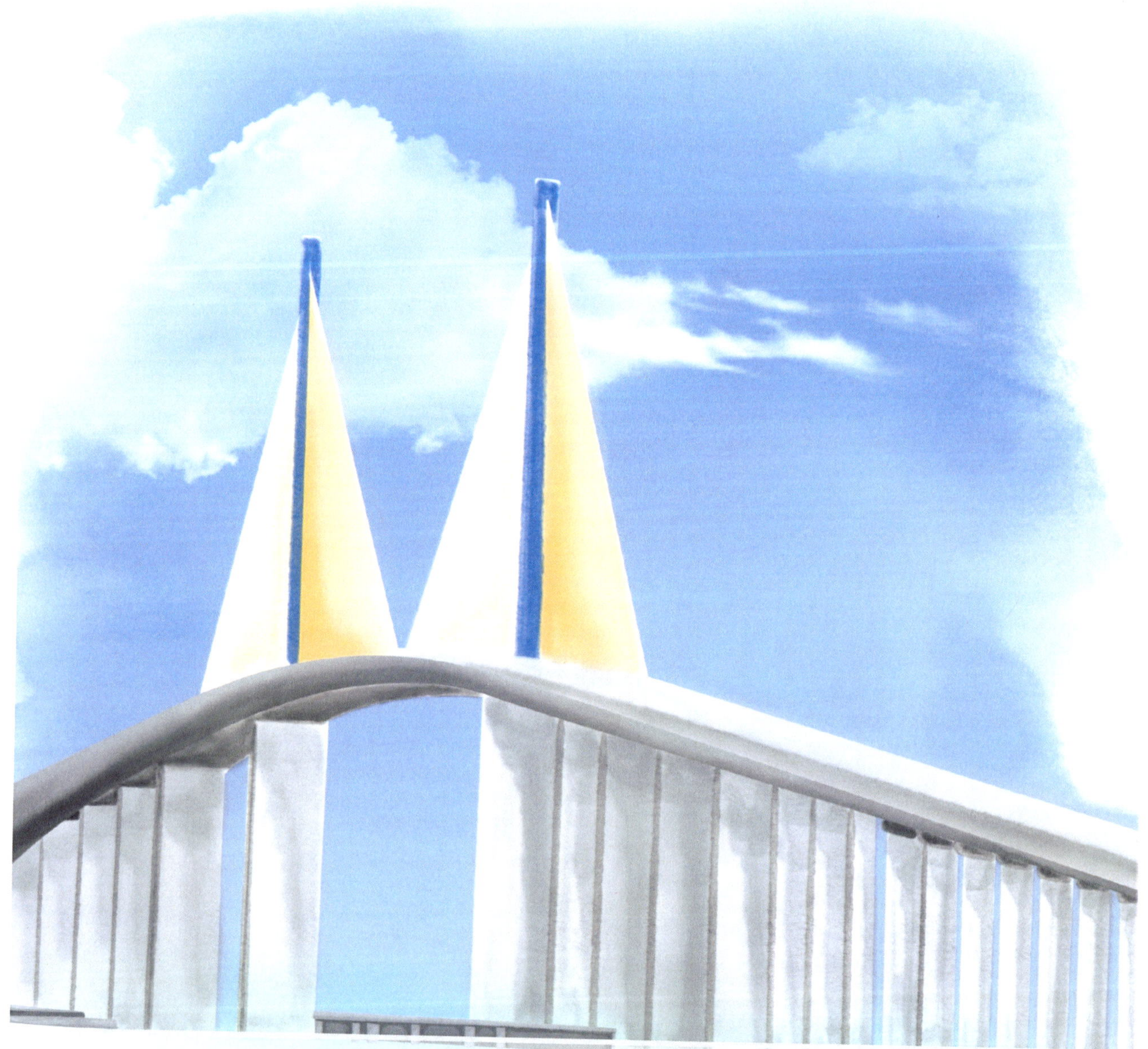

Another spectacular feature of St. Pete is the Sunshine Skyway Bridge. Spanning Lower Tampa Bay, it connects St. Pete with Manatee County to the south with cities like Sarasota and Bradenton. Whether you love or hate driving over the Skyway, it is a sight with its two tall cable towers that rise like great sails and the view from the bridge is breathtaking.

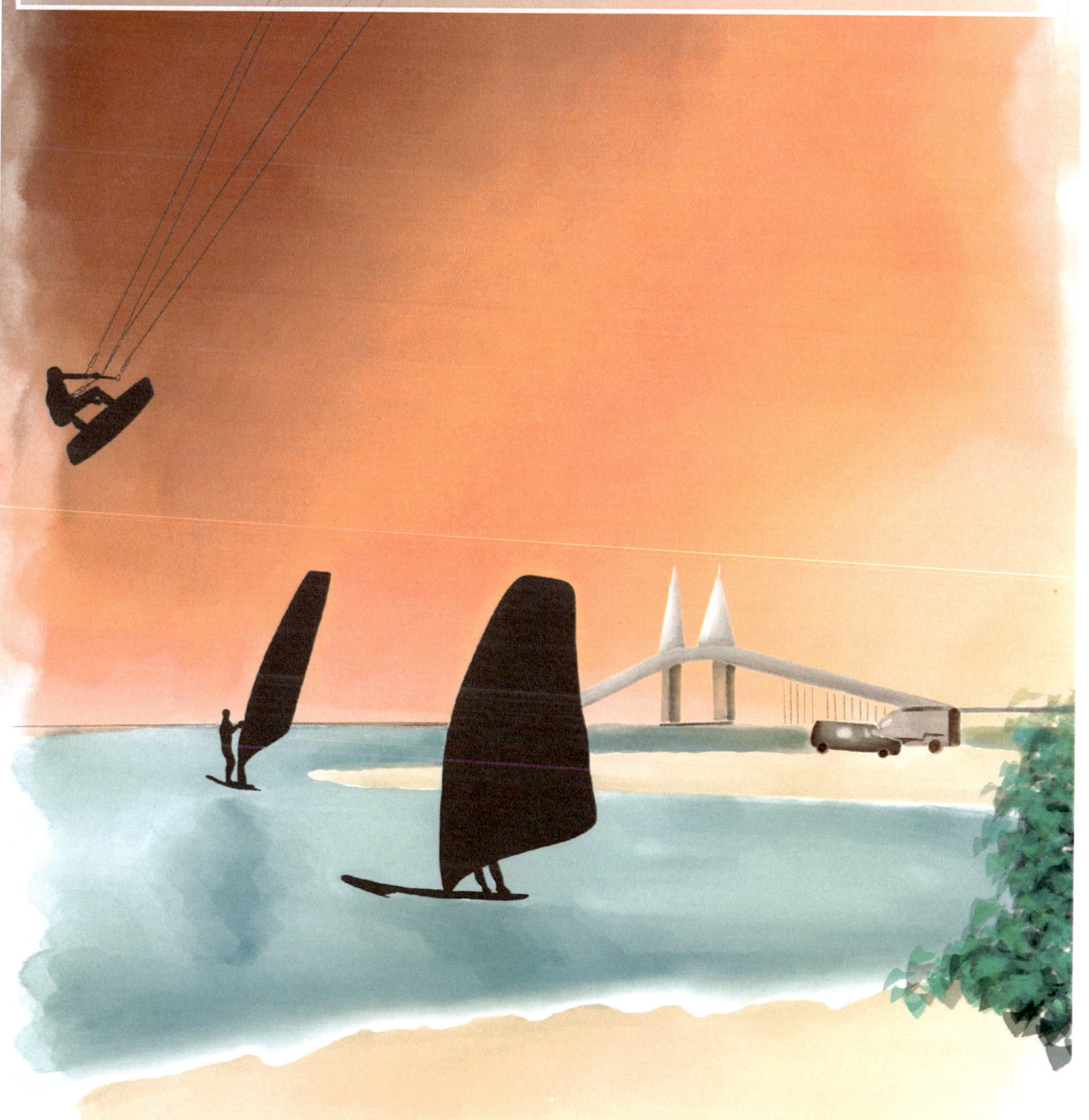

Play through, play on, play under, play near, the Landscape, bay and Gulf are amazing!

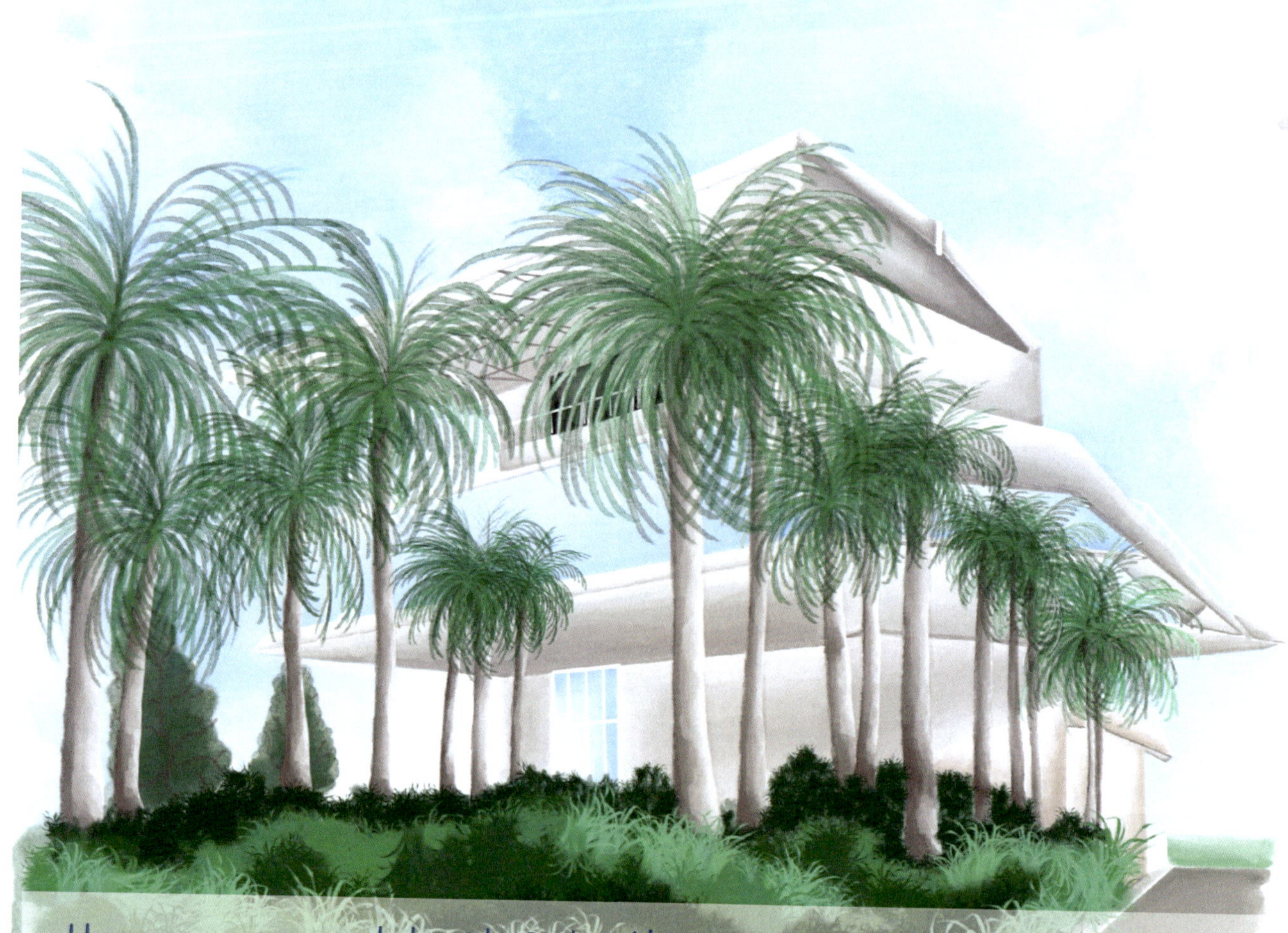

How ever you get to St. Pete, the St. Pete Pier is a great place to start your journey. From on-going local craft bazaars, to restaurants and even a beach, the pier is a destination itself. The St. Petersburg Municipal Marina is a fantastic place to catch a dolphin sight-seeing trip. Want to learn more about St. Pete? The St. Petersburg Museum of History is right there as well.

Not far from the pier is the Vinoy Marina. With the Vinoy Hotel in the backdrop, the marina hosts sailboats and mega yachts. Whether you need a place to dock or just a place to dream, the marina is a beautiful place for both. (Oh, and the Vinoy might just be haunted!)

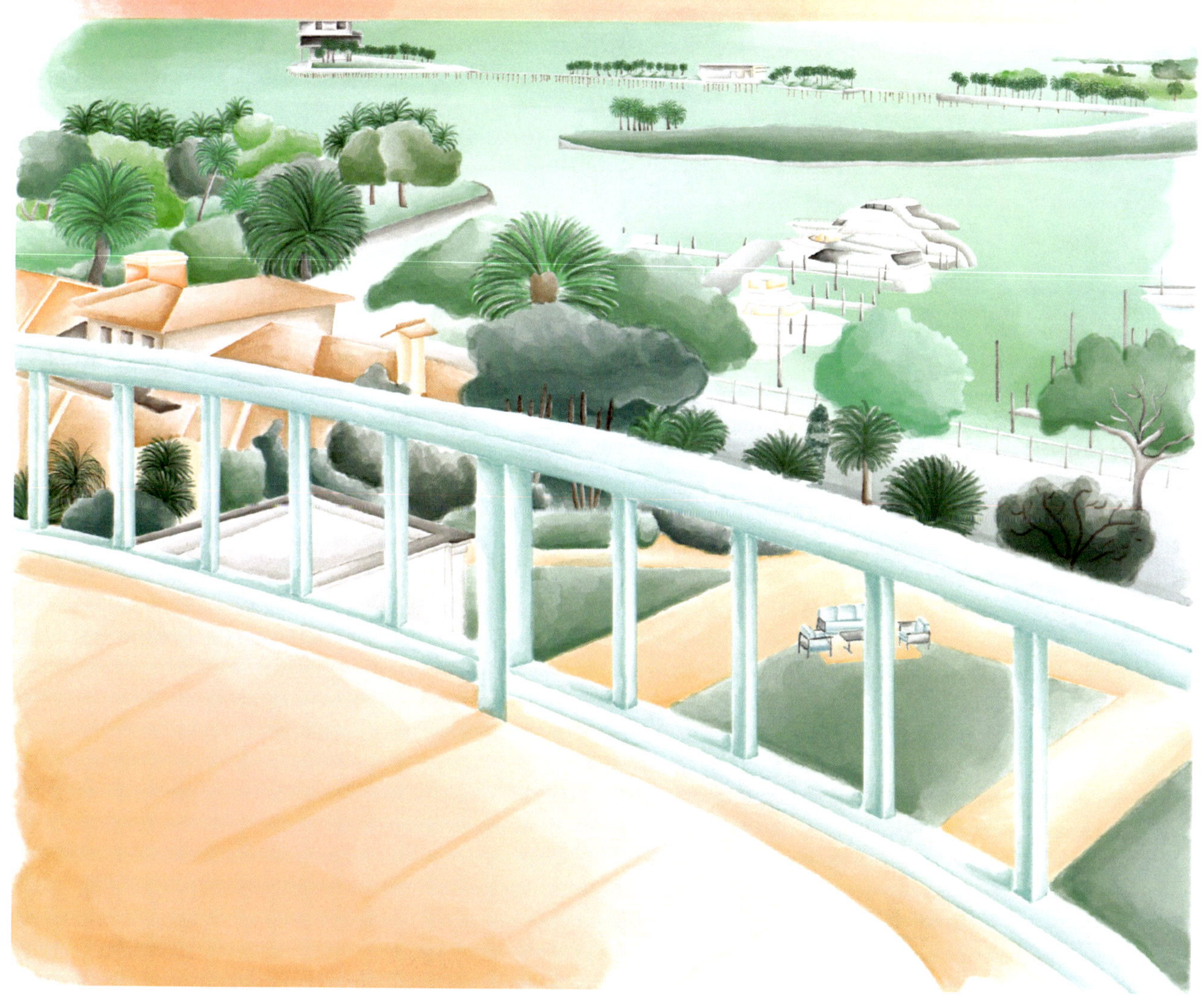

On the other side of the St. Pete Pier is Coast Guard Sector St. Petersburg, which shares a peninsula with the Albert Whitted Public Airport. With a coastline and bays as busy as St. Pete's, keeping people safe on the water is a full-time job.

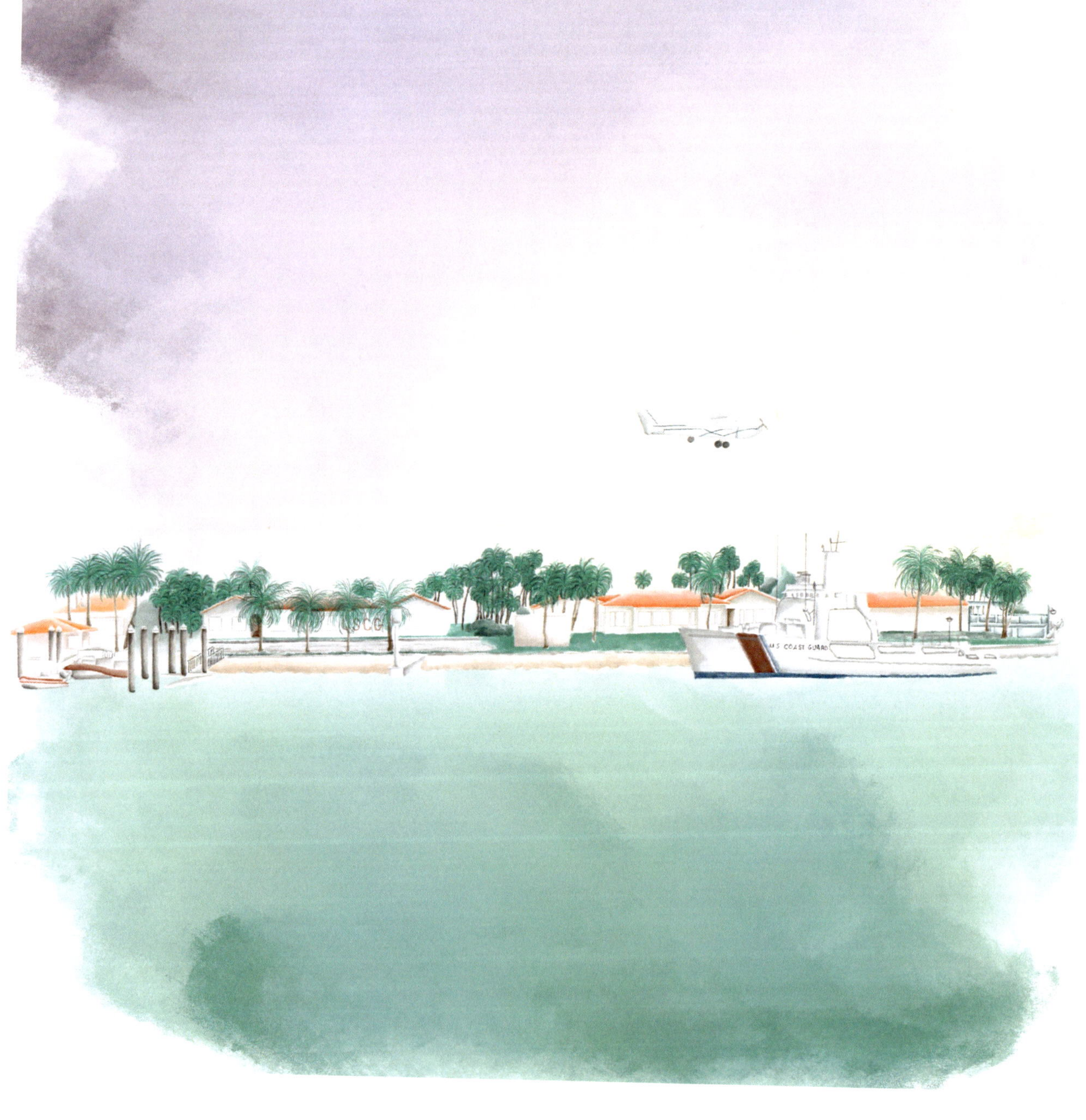

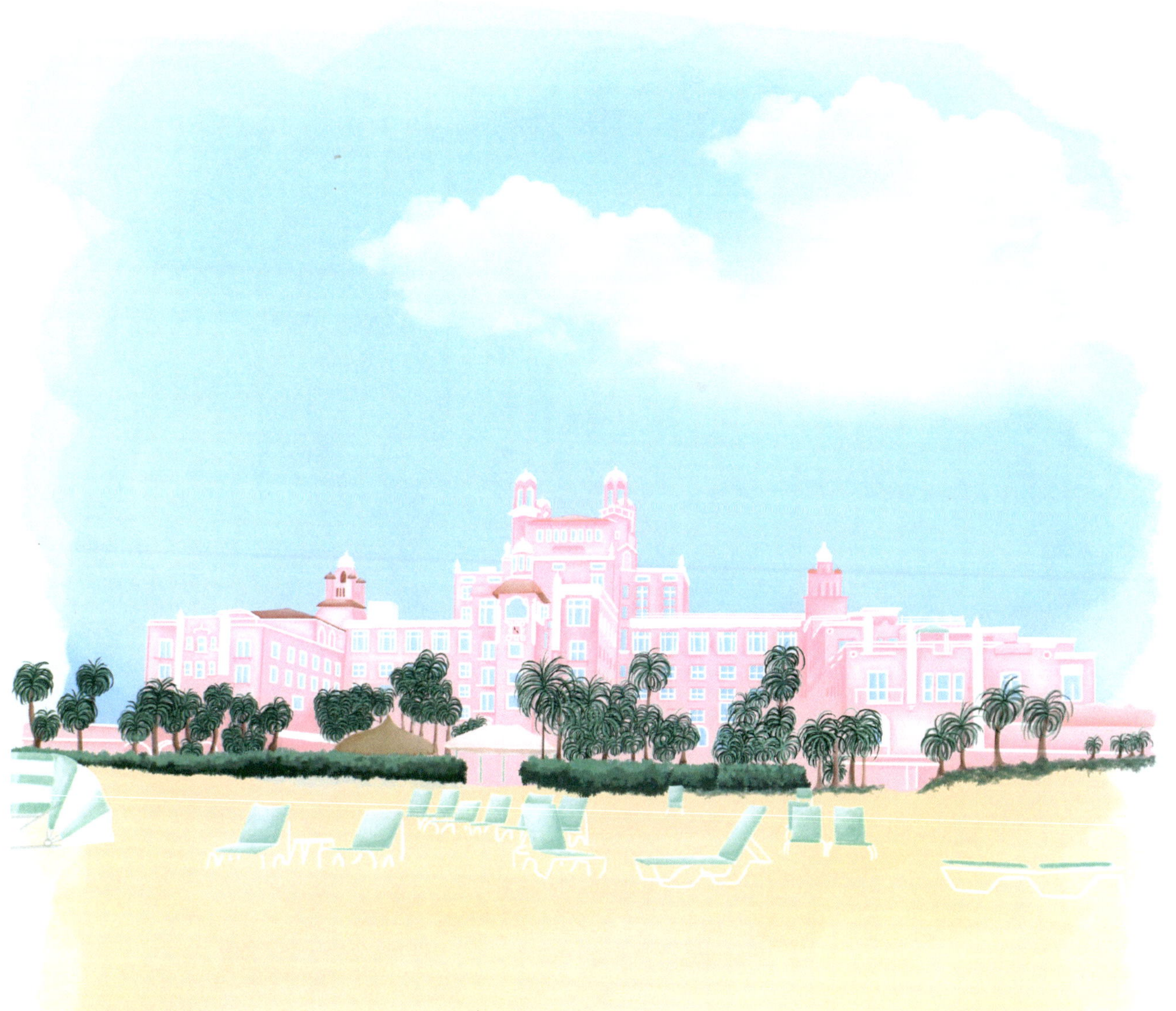

The Don CeSar Hotel or "Pink Lady" is a St. Pete Beach icon. Since it opened in 1928, it has played host to guests, movie stars and destination weddings. Perched right on a magnificent stretch of beach, it is a perfect vacation and sunset-chasing spot. Oh, and like the Vinoy, rumor is, some guests loved it so much, they never left. Boo!

Located not far down the road is Spinners Rooftop Grille. Sitting twelve-stories high above the shoreline at The Bellwether Hotel, you can dine with a 360-degree view. Don't worry about craning your neck to see, the dining room floor spins. Just sit back and enjoy the view as it comes around.

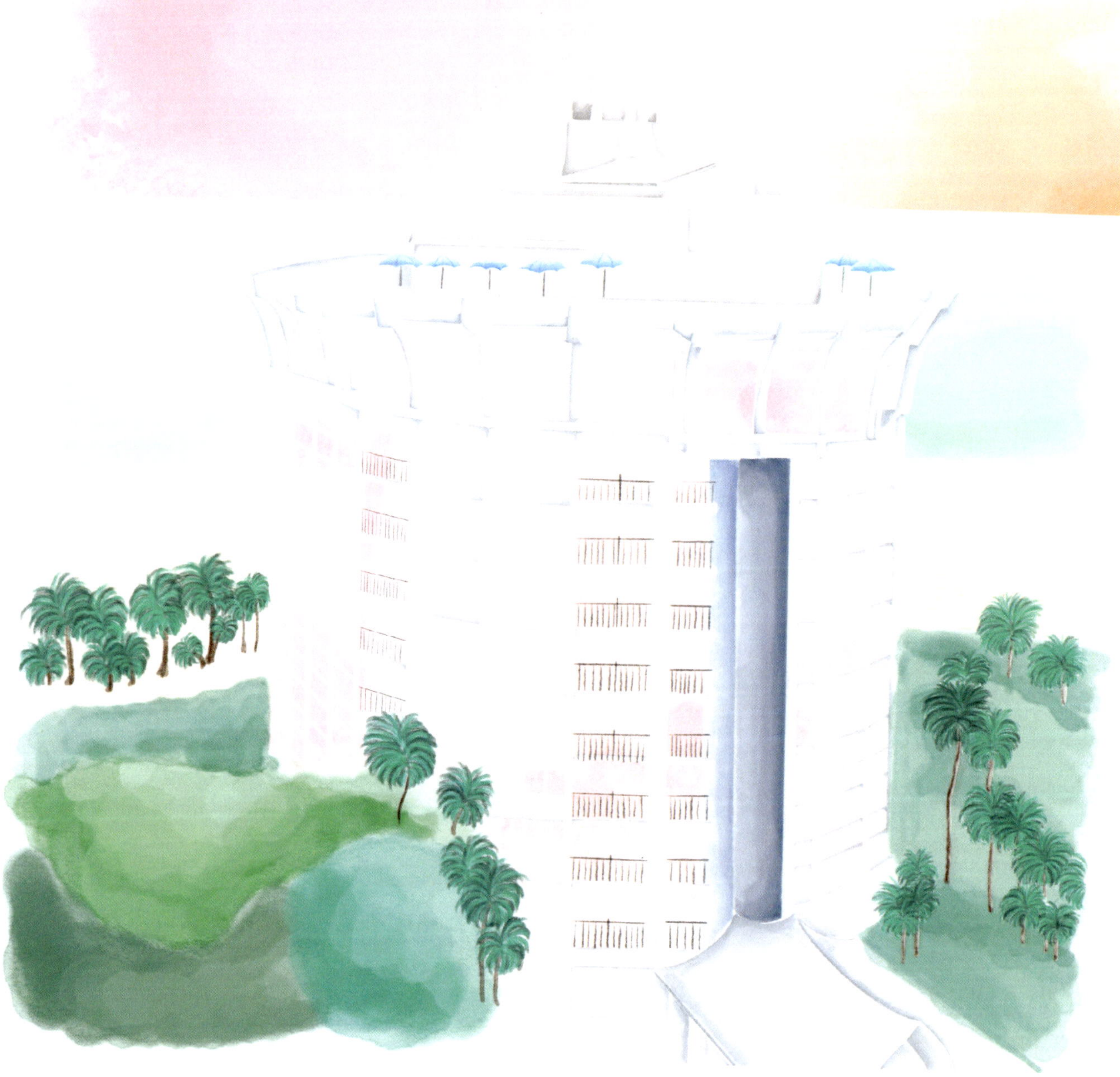

Sitting on Mullet Key, Fort DeSoto Park hosts campsites, boat launches, nature trails, amazing fishing and stunning beaches. The best part of Fort DeSoto's beaches, they are homes to loggerhead sea turtles. If you are lucky (and very careful), you could witness nesting turtles or even the little ones making their way into surf as they say hello to the world.

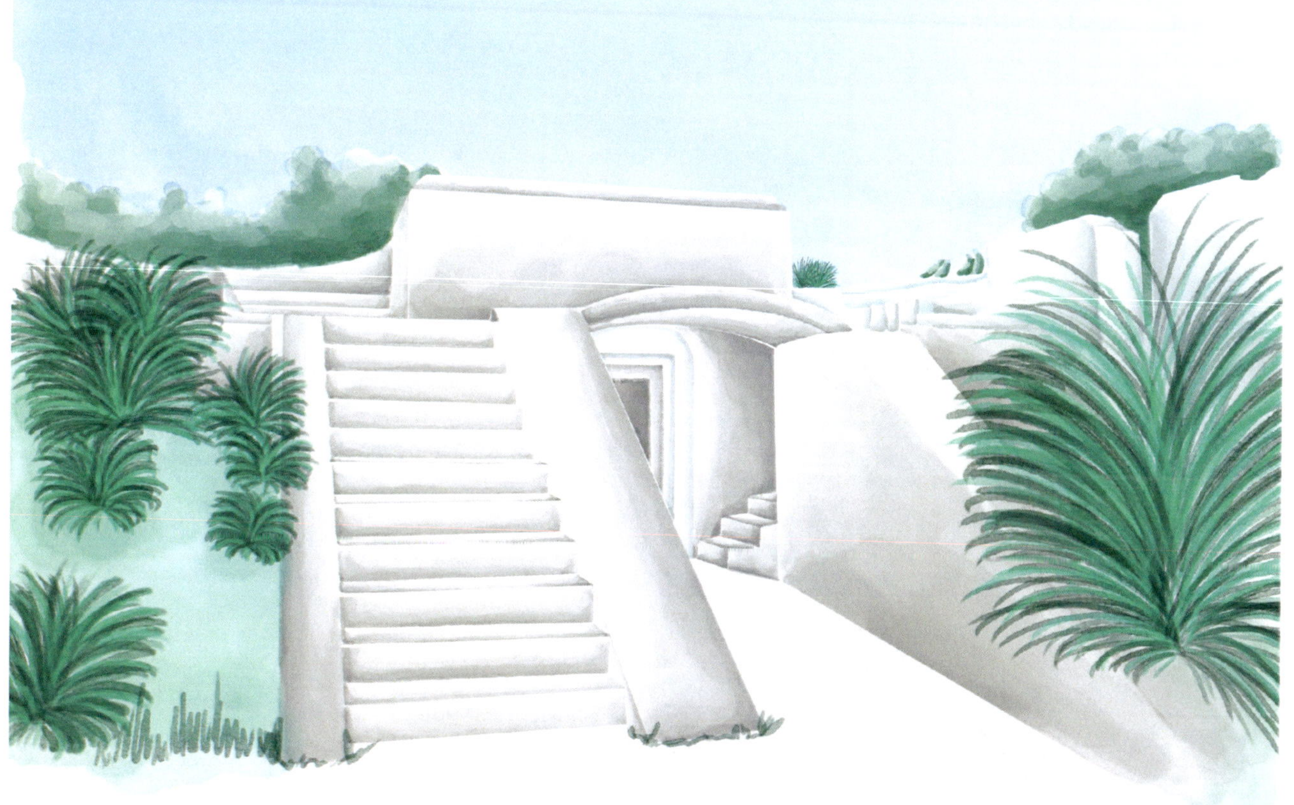

Tierra Verde is an island or actually a collection of islands near the entrance to Tampa Bay. Named for its lush beauty, it is an oasis on the clear waters where the Gulf meets the bay. For fun, there are pools with swim-up bars you can play in as you visit at some of the hotels.

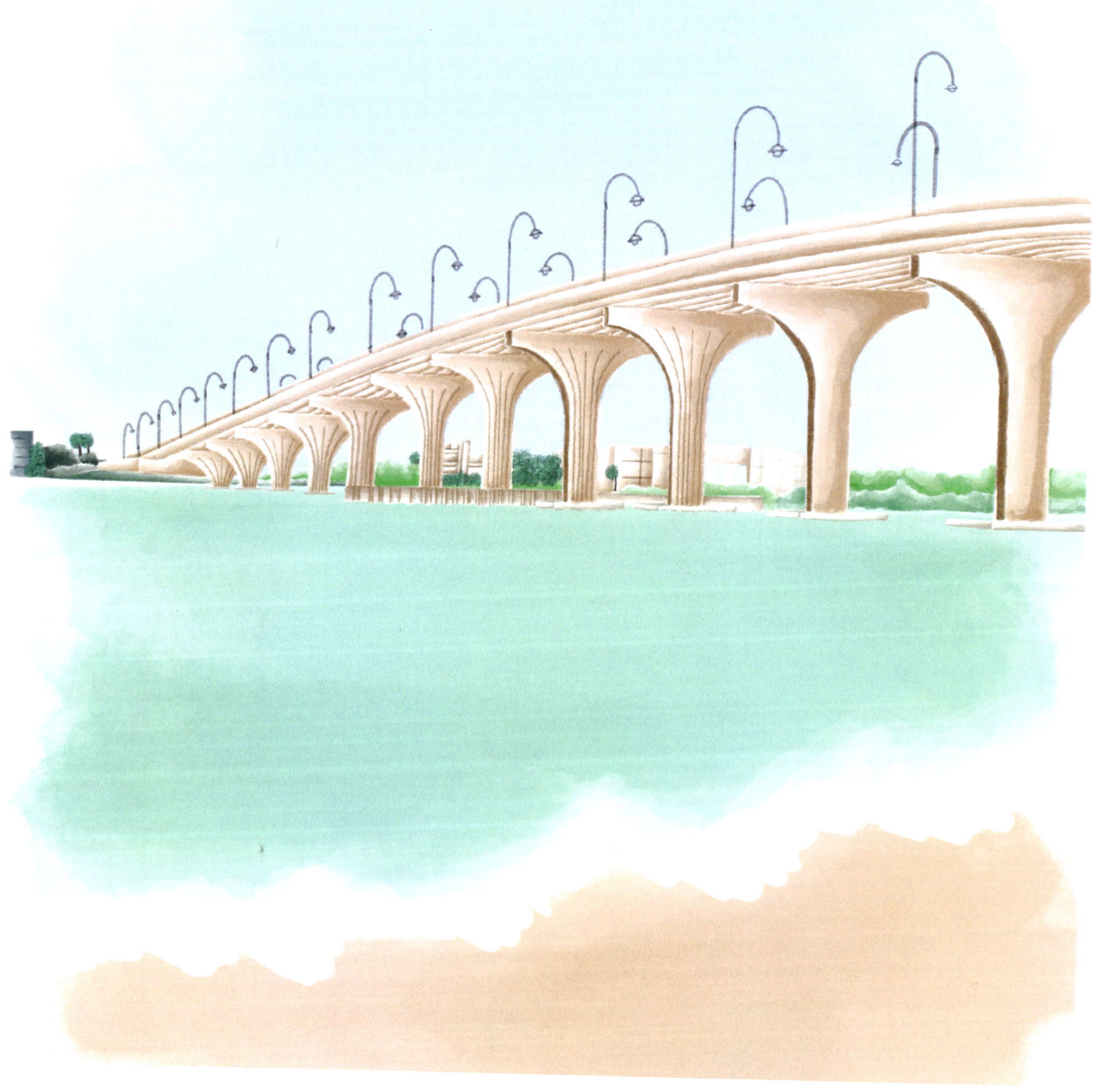

Shell Key is an uninhabited barrier island accessible by boat or ferry. Want to camp on an island under the stars while waves lap gently against the shore? You can at Shell Key. Like Fort DeSoto, Shell Key is a great place to spy nesting sea turtles. And of course, sea shells.

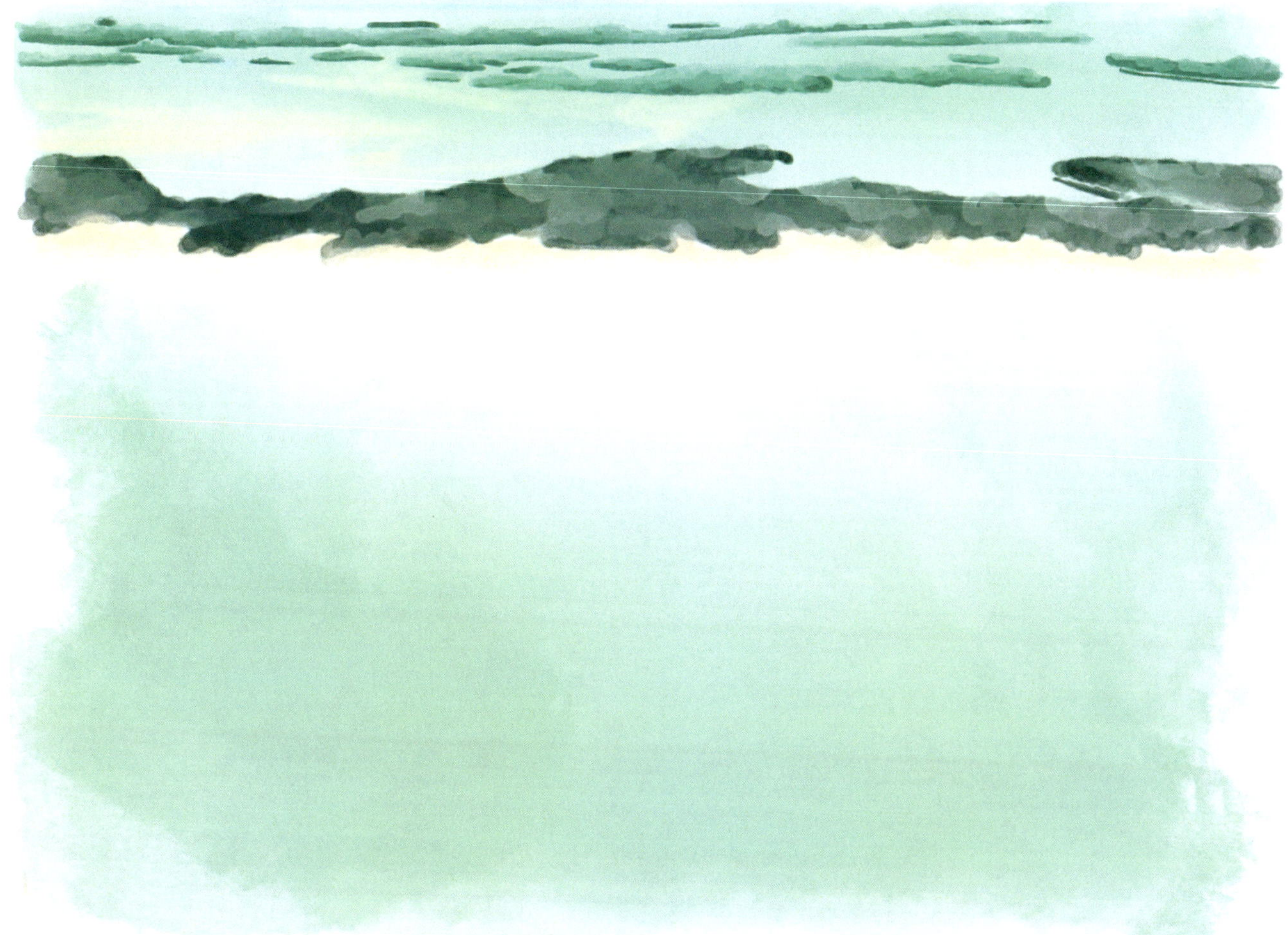

Home to grand mansions, historic golf courses and shaped like an elephant's trunk, Snell Isle is a great place to live, relax, jog and watch for manatees. See the sea cow's resemblance to beautiful, mythical mermaids? Yeah, I don't either, but they are beautiful in their own, sweet, gentle, sea grass-chomping way.

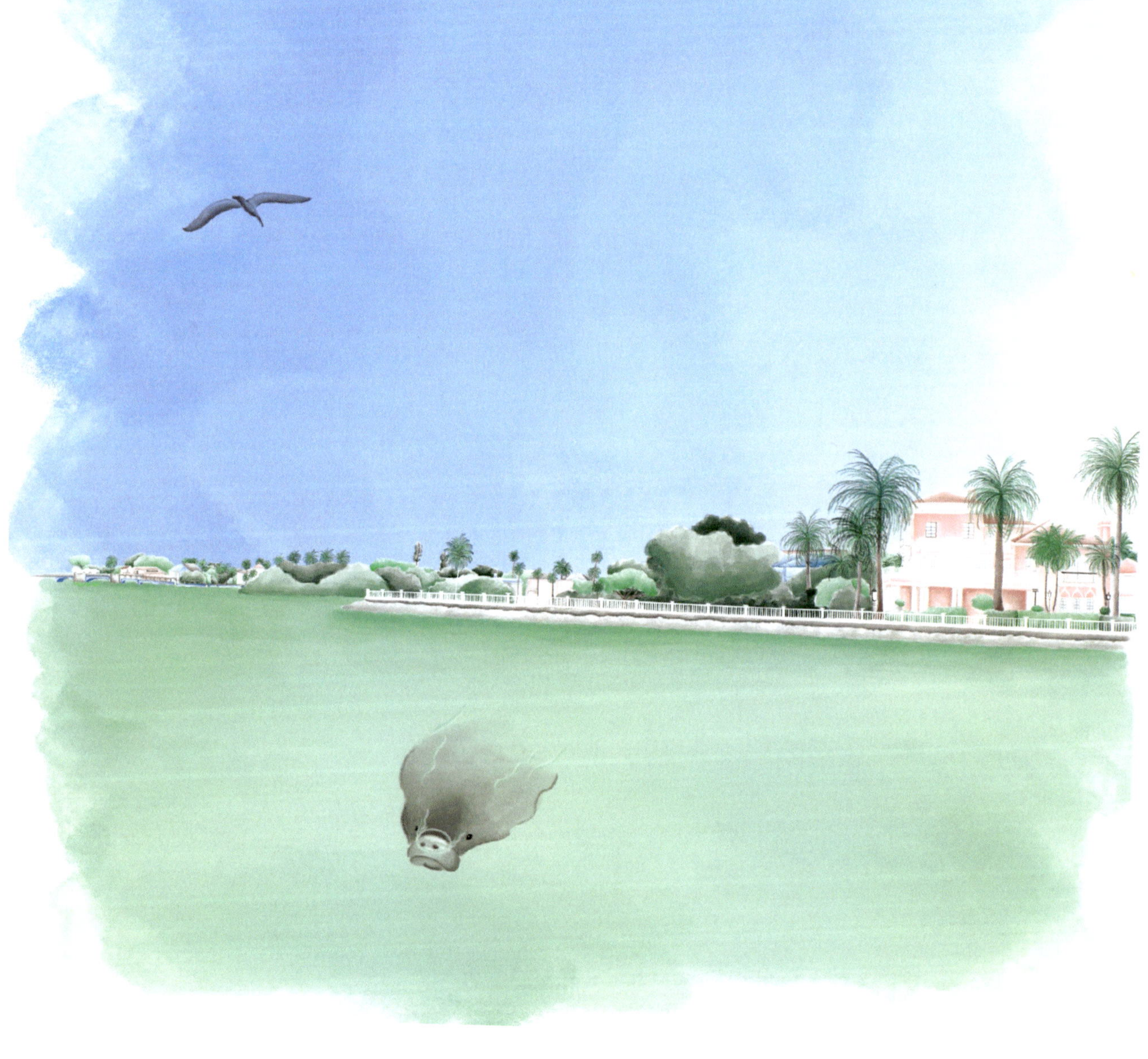

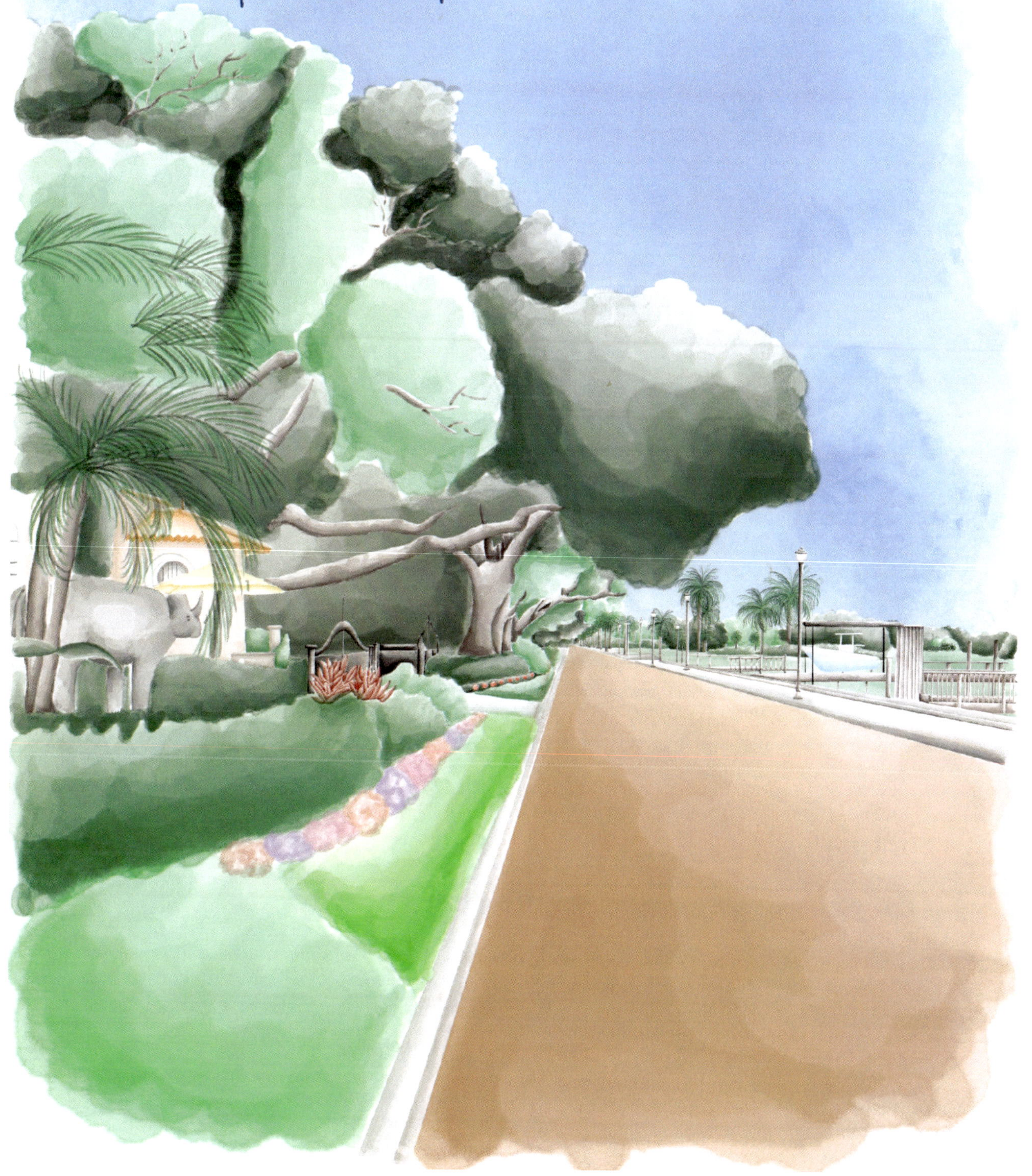

Coffee Pot Bayou is a quiet, tranquil place to relax, spy manatees, bike, jog, or just sit on a park bench and realize how spectacular life is in St. Pete.

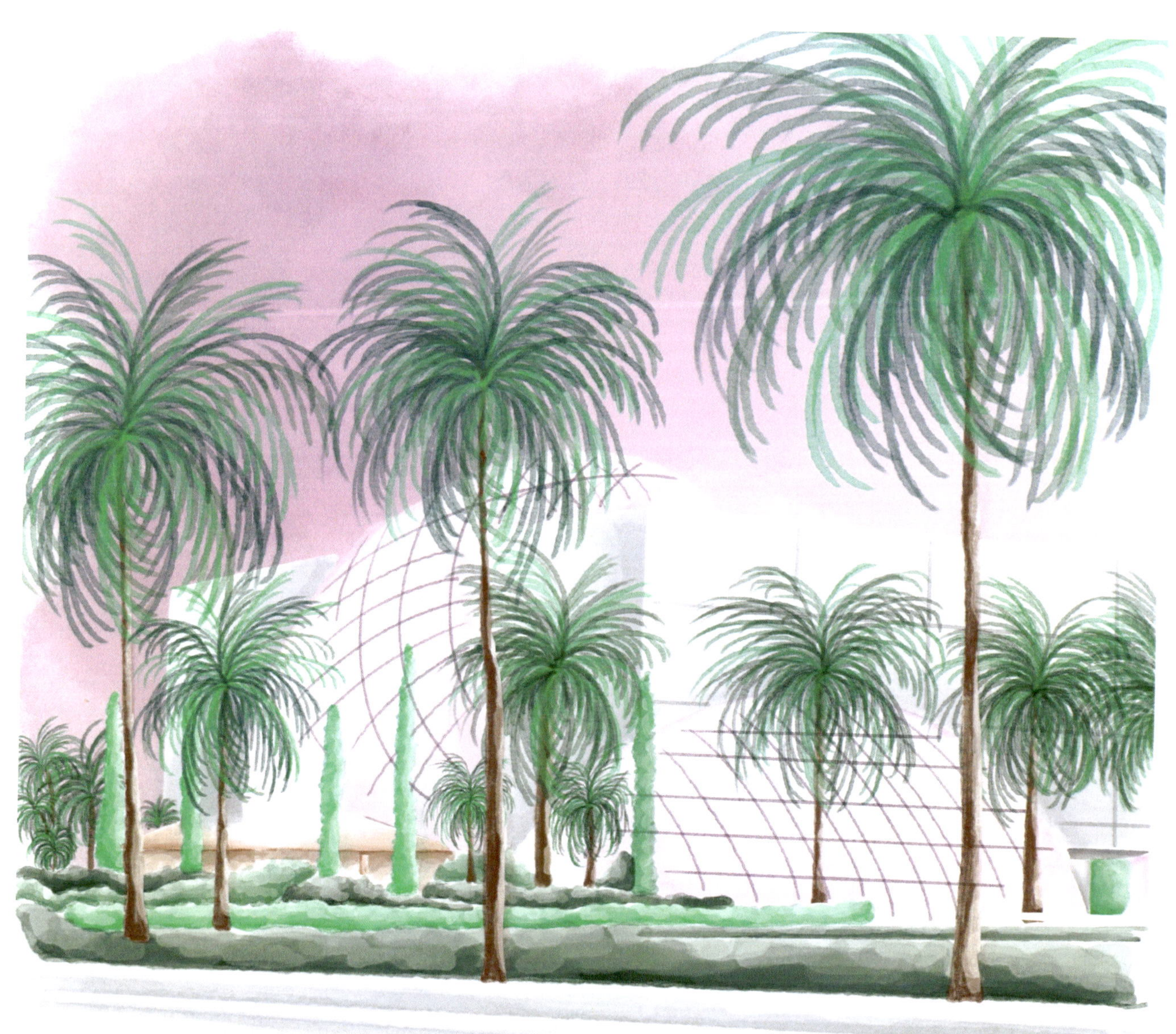

Aside from the water and beaches, St. Pete is acclaimed as an art town. From local painters and galleries to museums like the Dali Museum, the Chihuly Collection and the Museum of Fine Art, you can study works by Monet, Rodin and O'Keeffe. There is even a museum all about American Arts and Crafts.

Sunken Gardens is a must-stop for anyone who visits
St. Pete. Lush gardens and trails are filled with exotic tropical
plants. Huge royal palms, rainbow eucalyptus trees, and
Southern live oaks are a big part of the drama. But the star
of the show is the flock of flamingos so pink that the Vinoy
and The Don CeSar would be jealous. Come on. It's Florida.
You gotta hang with some flamingos.

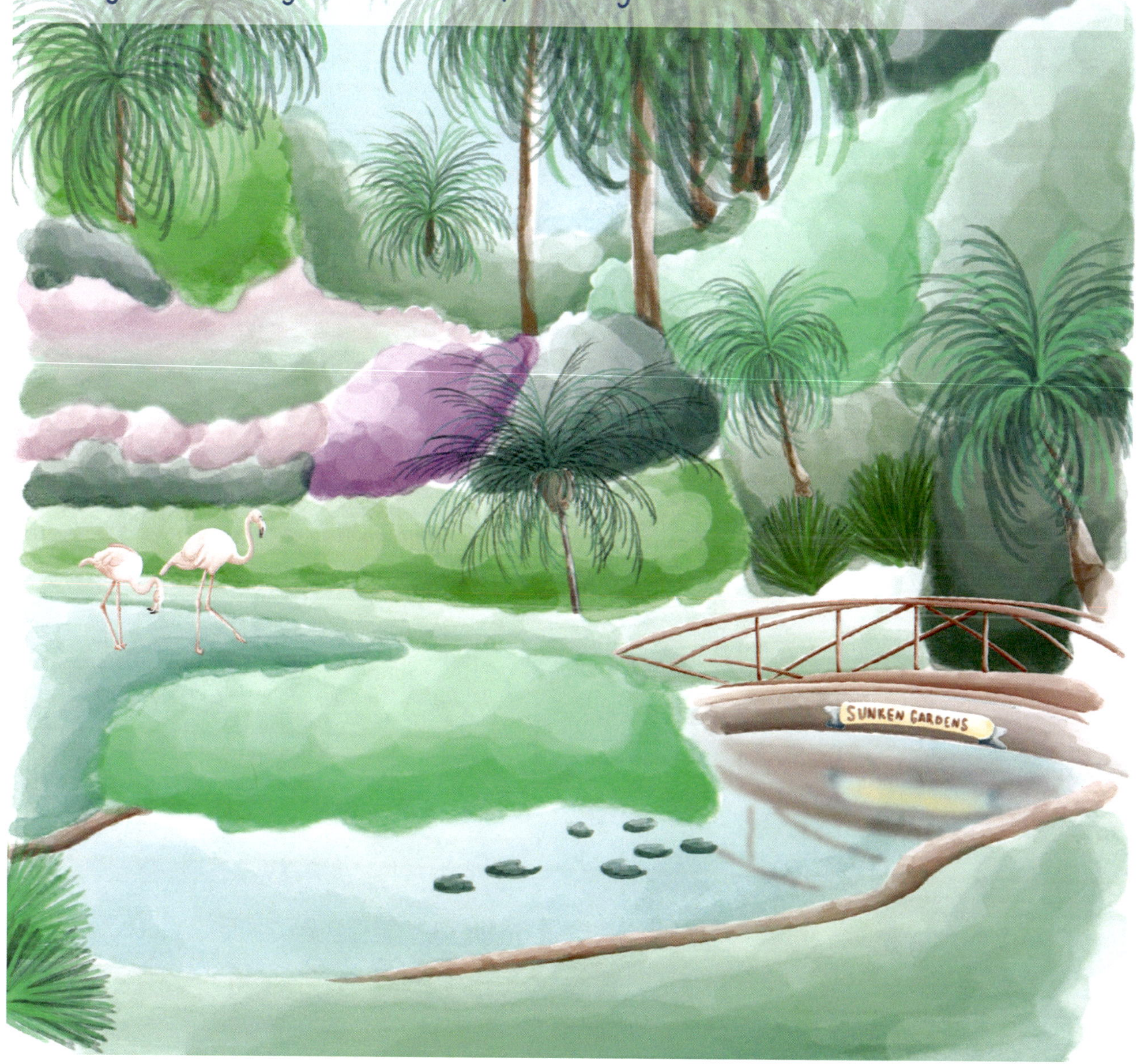

Located on the grounds of the St. Pete High School is the Sunday Market. It is a weekly bazaar with wares from local artists, small businesses and mouth-watering food trucks. The challenge is choosing which vendor to visit first...

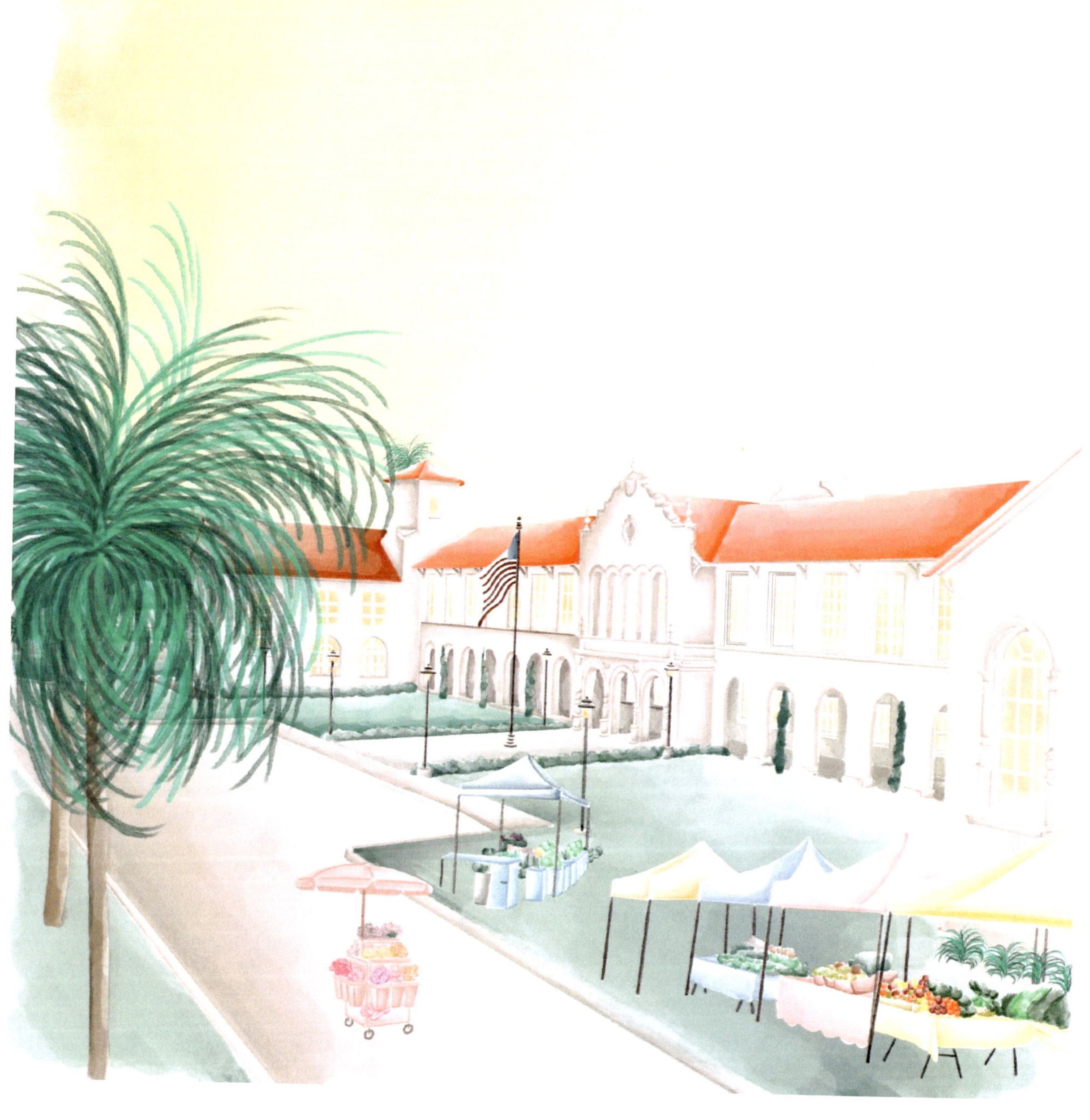

Speaking of reels, fishing off the pier, on the beach or in a boat is a relaxing way to catch your dinner or just have some fun. One of the few things you can fail at and still say you had a great time, but really, the fish around St. Pete are plentiful.

Did I mention dolphins a few times? I could watch them for hours. You can see them from shore, from the bridges and on a dolphin tour. A lot of times, they'll even hitch a ride on your wake for some fun themselves.

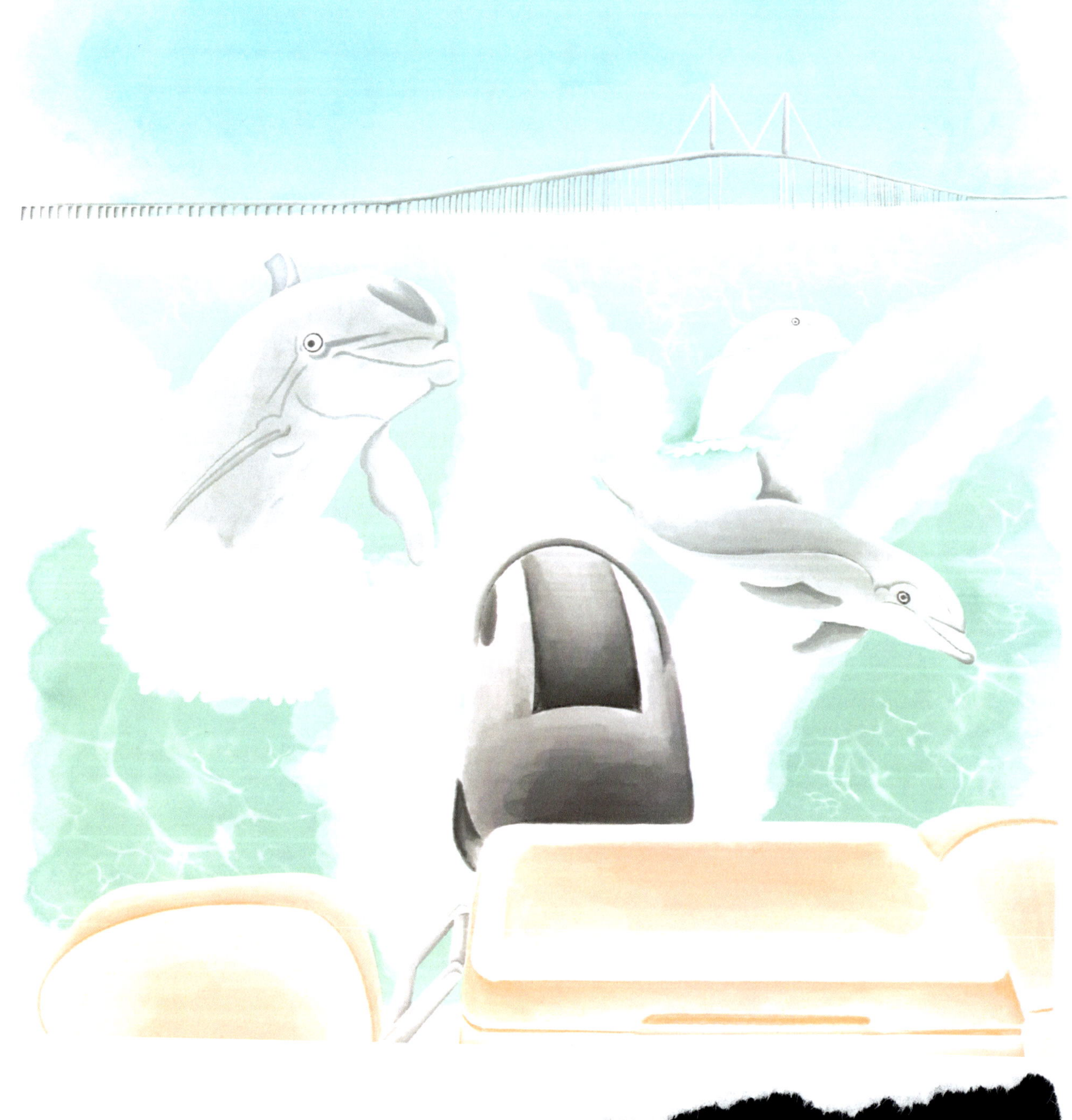

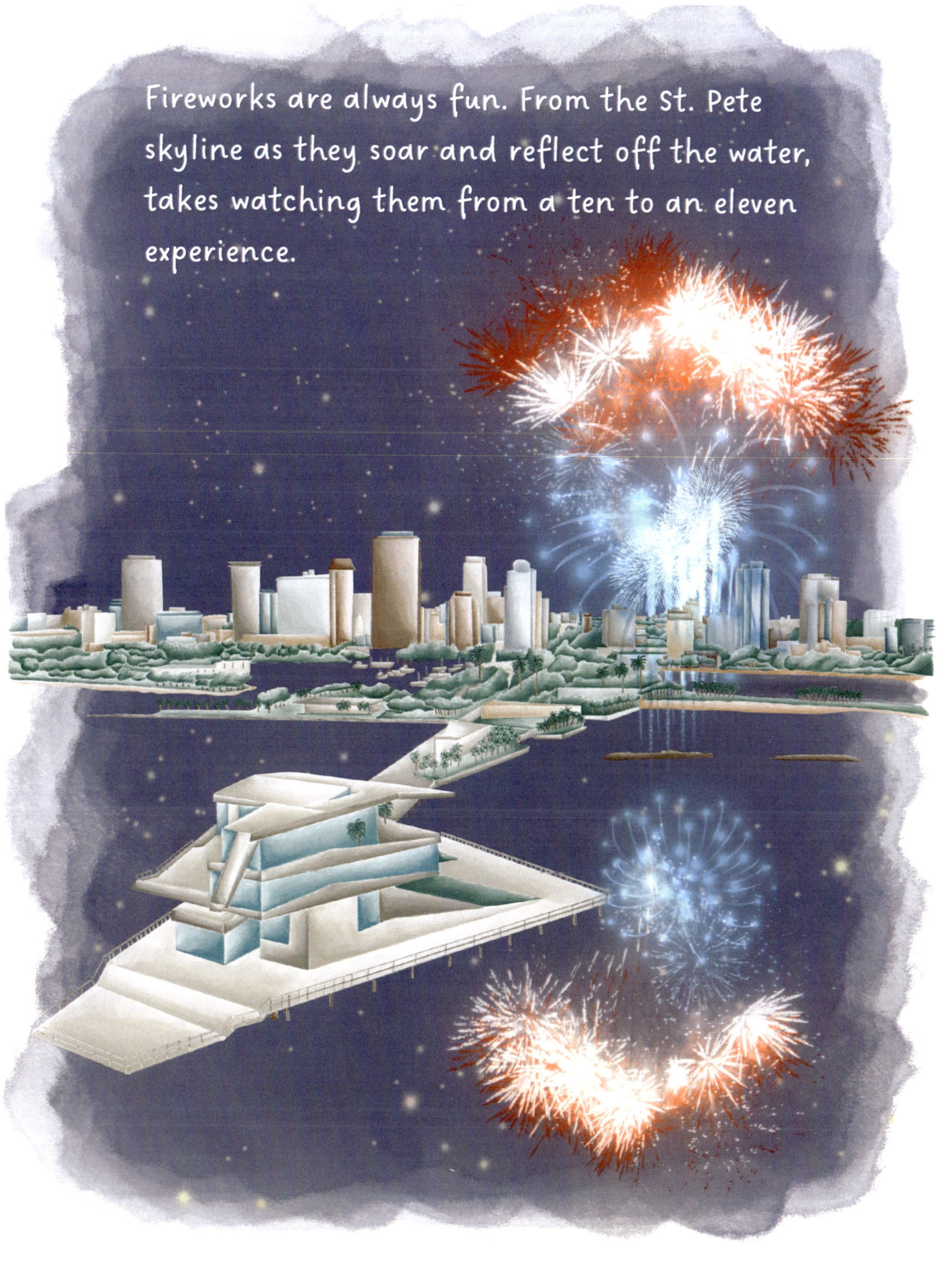

Fireworks are always fun. From the St. Pete skyline as they soar and reflect off the water, takes watching them from a ten to an eleven experience.

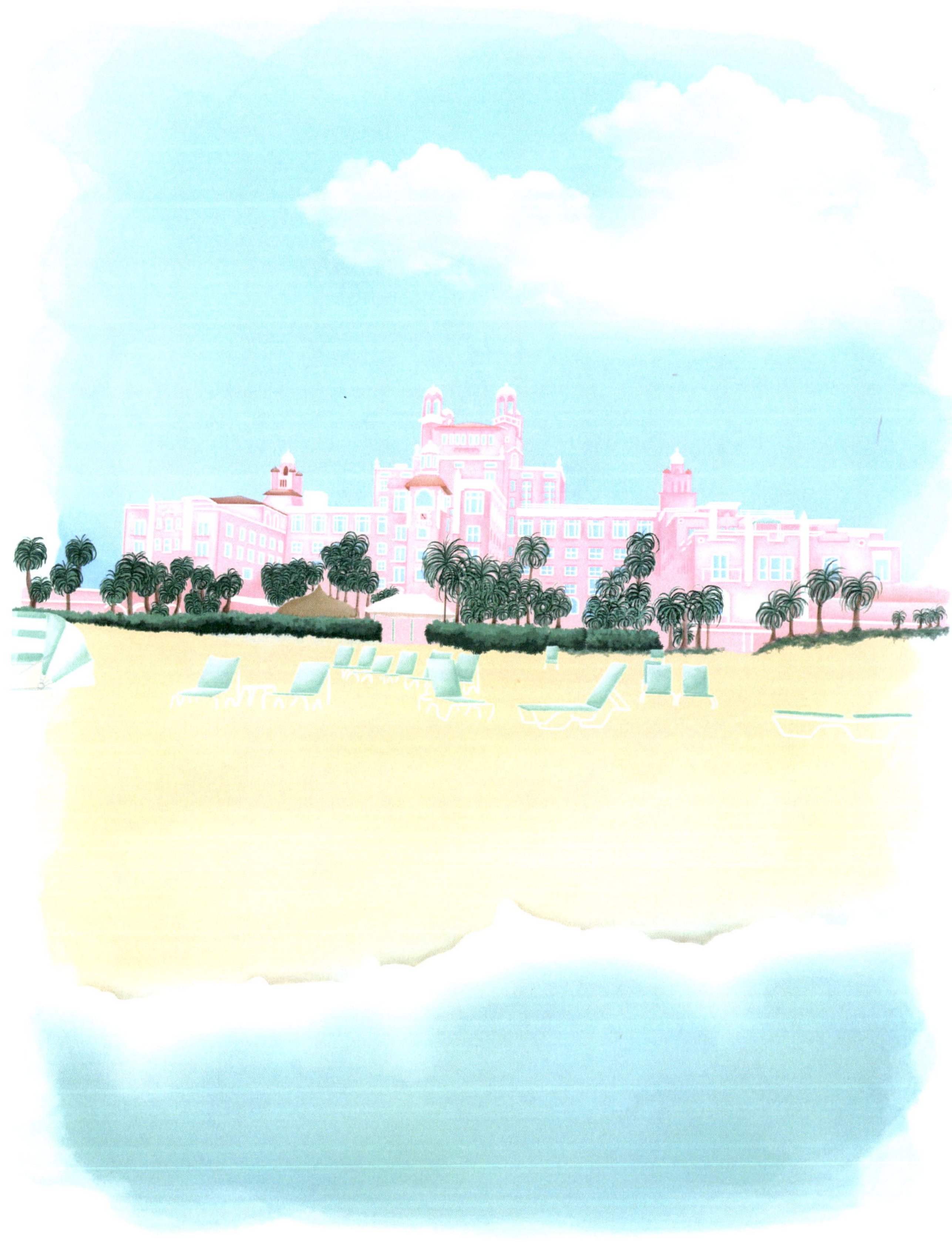

About the Author

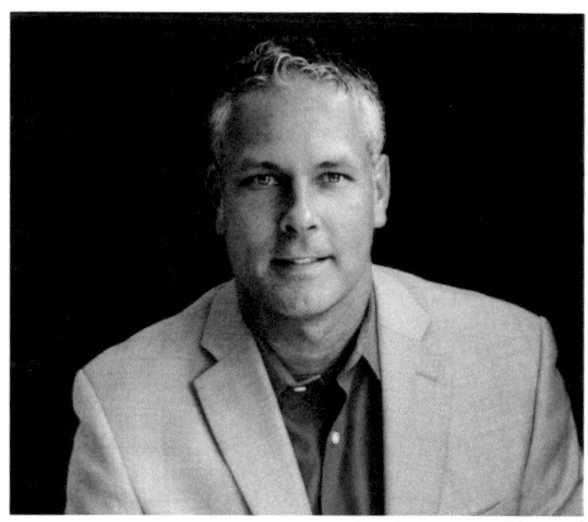

Seth is a serial entrepreneur, adventurer and author. His thriller novels include *Penance, Penance: Unredeemable, Penance: Absolution, Patriot X, Patriot X: Insurrection, Dark Chase, Dark Chase: Dead Run.* His Beach House Mysteries series include *Trouble on Treasure Island, A Caper on Carolina Beach* and *Peril on Palm Beach.* His Christmas collection includes *Finding Christmas, The Tree Farm, The Nativity, The Toy Store, The Christmas Café* and *Love at the Christmas Con.* His children's books include *Letters from Santa, The Hollow, The Cryptid Rangers* series he wrote with his son and the *Hurricane Channing series.* Seth partners with Hire Heroes USA dedicating volunteer hours in conjunction with his Patriot X series. *The Christmas Café* supports Hallmark and Great American Family actress Jen Lilley's Christmas is Not Cancelled charity programs as well as Jill Wagner's The Patriotic Pick.

About the Illustrator

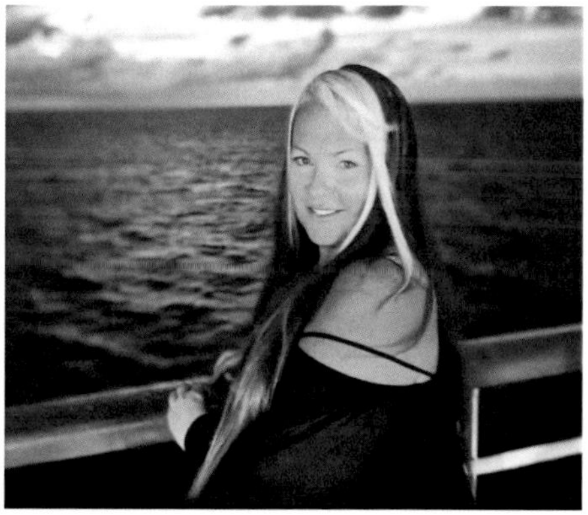

Michele grew up in the Pacific Northwest and now resides in Florida near her 3 grown children and one grandbaby. She has always had a fondness for the sea, as well as tropical flora and fauna. Her passion for painting the beach and the beauty of it began early on, giving her the curiosity to experiment with oils and acrylics. Illustrating children's books was recently introduced to her and she accepted it as a new challenge and passion! In fact, every page of Hurricane Channing and the Christmas Puppy was its own oil painting! Switching from paintbrushes and oils to digital drawing has been the greatest recent challenge, but she accepted it and eagerly waits for the next story to bring to life! Michele has also written and illustrated her own children's book series Boots the Dog!

Other Books by Seth

Beach House Mysteries Series

Trouble on Treasure Island

A Caper on Carolina Beach

Peril in Palm Beach

Cursed in Cape Fear

Other Titles

Penance

Penance: Unredeemable

Penance: Absolution

Penance: Awakening

Dark Chase

Dark Chase: Dead Run

Dark Chase: Beast

Patriot X

Patriot X: Insurrection

Other Children's Books by Seth

Hurricane Channing and the Lost Flamingo

Hurricane Channing and the Mommy Manatee

Hurricane Channing and the Daily Dolphin

Hurricane Channing and the Christmas Puppy

Hurricane Channing and the Halloween Bat

Letters from Santa

The Heart of a Reindeer

Cryptid Rangers: Secret of the Skunk Ape

Cryptid Rangers: Beast of Bladenboro

The Hollow

The *Too* Helpful Little Angel

Holiday Books by Seth

Finding Christmas

The Nativity

The Tree Farm

The Toy Store

The Christmas Café

Love at the Christmas Con

A Southern Charm Christmas

A Roadhouse Christmas

Other Books by Michele

Hurricane Channing and the Lost Flamingo

Hurricane Channing and the Mommy Manatee

Hurricane Channing and the Daily Dolphin

Hurricane Channing and the Christmas Puppy

Hurricane Channing and the Halloween Bat

The Heart of a Reindeer

The *Too* Helpful Little Angel

Southport Summers

Boots and the Runaway Dog

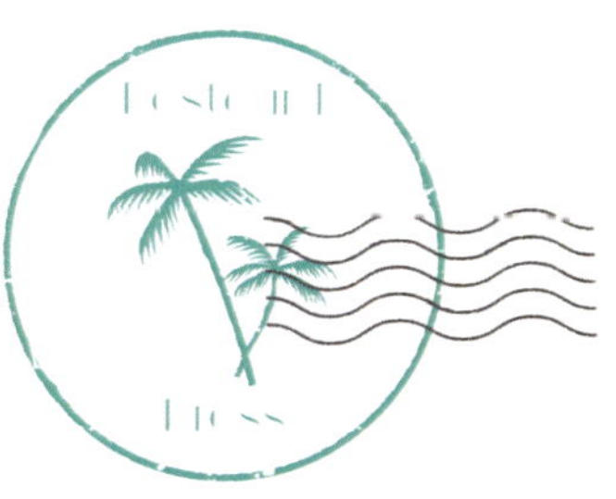

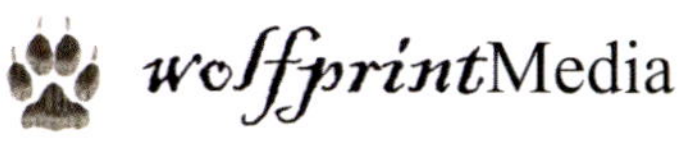